D1414631

"It's hard to connect with your child without f
As counselors and speakers at parenting ever
a great deal of time teaching parents about d
child is—not just physically, but emotionally, s
to truly know and understand *who* your child
key to connecting. The Phase Guides give you the tools to do just that. Our wise
friends Reggie and Kristen have put together an insightful, hopeful, practical,
and literal year-by-year guide that will help you to understand and connect with
your child at every age."

**SISSY GOFF**
*M.ED., LPC-MHSP, DIRECTOR OF CHILD & ADOLESCENT COUNSELING AT DAYSTAR
COUNSELING MINISTRIES IN NASHVILLE, TENNESSEE, SPEAKER AND AUTHOR OF
ARE MY KIDS ON TRACK?*

"These resources for parents are fantastically empowering, absolute in their
simplicity, and completely doable in every way. The hard work that has gone
into the Phase Project will echo through the next generation of children in
powerful ways."

**JENNIFER WALKER**
*RN BSN, AUTHOR AND FOUNDER OF MOMS ON CALL*

"We all know where we want to end up in our parenting, but how to get there
can seem like an unsolved mystery. Through the Phase Project series, Reggie
Joiner and Kristen Ivy team up to help us out. The result is a resource that guides
us through the different seasons of raising children, and provides a road map to
parenting in such a way that we finish up with very few regrets."

**SANDRA STANLEY**
*FOSTER CARE ADVOCATE, BLOGGER, WIFE TO ANDY STANLEY, MOTHER OF THREE*

"Not only are the Phase Guides the most creative and well-thought-out guides
to parenting I have ever encountered, these books are ESSENTIAL to my
daily parenting. With a 13-year-old, 11-year-old, and 9-year-old at home, I am
swimming in their wake of daily drama and delicacy. These books are a reminder
to enjoy every second. Because it's just a phase."

**CARLOS WHITTAKER**
*AUTHOR, SPEAKER, FATHER OF THREE*

"As the founder of Minnie's Food Pantry, I see thousands of people each
month with children who will benefit from the advice, guidance, and nuggets
of information on how to celebrate and understand the phases of their child's
life. Too often we feel like we're losing our mind when sweet little Johnny
starts to change his behavior into a person we do not know. I can't wait to start
implementing the principles of these books with my clients to remind them . . .
it's just a phase."

**CHERYL JACKSON**
*FOUNDER OF MINNIE'S FOOD PANTRY, AWARD-WINNING PHILANTHROPIST,
AND GRANDMOTHER*

"I began exploring this resource with my counselor hat on, thinking how valuable this will be for the many parents I spend time with in my office. I ended up taking my counselor hat off and putting on my parent hat. Then I kept thinking about friends who are teachers, coaches, youth pastors, and children's ministers, who would want this in their hands. What a valuable resource the Orange team has given us to better understand and care for the kids and adolescents we love. I look forward to sharing it broadly."

## DAVID THOMAS
*LMSW, DIRECTOR OF FAMILY COUNSELING, DAYSTAR COUNSELING MINISTRIES, SPEAKER AND AUTHOR OF* ARE MY KIDS ON TRACK? *AND* WILD THINGS: THE ART OF NURTURING BOYS

"I have always wished someone would hand me a manual for parenting. Well, the Phase Guides are more than what I wished for. They guide, inspire, and challenge me as a parent—while giving me incredible insight into my children at each age and phase. Our family will be using these every year!"

## COURTNEY DEFEO
*AUTHOR OF* IN THIS HOUSE, WE WILL GIGGLE, *MOTHER OF TWO*

"As I speak to high school students and their parents, I always wonder to myself: What would it have been like if they had better seen what was coming next? What if they had a guide that would tell them what to expect and how to be ready? What if they could anticipate what is predictable about the high school years before they actually hit? These Phase Guides give a parent that kind of preparation so they can have a plan when they need it most."

## JOSH SHIPP
*AUTHOR, TEEN EXPERT, AND YOUTH SPEAKER*

"The Phase Guides are incredibly creative, well researched, and filled with inspirational actions for everyday life. Each age-specific guide is catalytic for equipping parents to lead and love their kids as they grow up. I'm blown away and deeply encouraged by the content and by its creators. I highly recommend Phase resources for all parents, teachers, and influencers of children. This is the stuff that challenges us and changes our world. Get them. Read them. And use them!"

## DANIELLE STRICKLAND
*OFFICER WITH THE SALVATION ARMY, AUTHOR, SPEAKER, MOTHER OF TWO*

"It's true that parenting is one of life's greatest joys but it is not without its challenges. If we're honest, parenting can sometimes feel like trying to choreograph a dance to an ever-changing beat. It can be clumsy and riddled with well-meaning missteps. If parenting is a dance, this Parenting Guide is a skilled instructor refining your technique and helping you move gracefully to a steady beat. For those of us who love to plan ahead, this guide will help you anticipate what's to come so you can be poised and ready to embrace the moments you want to enjoy."

## TINA NAIDOO
*MSSW, LCSW EXECUTIVE DIRECTOR, THE POTTER'S HOUSE OF DALLAS, INC.*

# PARENTING YOUR KINDERGARTNER

## A GUIDE TO MAKING THE MOST OF THE "LOOK AT ME!" PHASE

KRISTEN IVY AND REGGIE JOINER

# PARENTING YOUR KINDERGARTNER
## A GUIDE TO MAKING THE MOST OF THE
## "LOOK AT ME!" PHASE

Published by Orange, a division of The reThink Group, Inc.,
5870 Charlotte Lane, Suite 300,
Cumming, GA 30040 U.S.A.

The Orange logo is a registered trademark of The reThink Group, Inc.
All rights reserved. Except for brief excerpts for review purposes, no part of
this book may be reproduced or used in any form without written permission
from the publisher.

All Scripture quotations, unless otherwise indicated, are taken from the Holy
Bible, New International Version®, NIV®. Copyright ©1973, 1978, 1984, 2011 by
Biblica, Inc.™ Used by permission of Zondervan. All rights reserved worldwide.
www.zondervan.com The "NIV" and "New International Version" are trademarks
registered in the United States Patent and Trademark Office by Biblica, Inc.™

©2017 The Phase Project
Authors: Kristen Ivy and Reggie Joiner
Lead Editor: Karen Wilson
Editing Team: Melanie Williams, Hannah Crosby, Sherry Surratt

Art Direction: Ryan Boon and Hannah Crosby
Book Design: FiveStone and Sharon van Rossum
Project Manager : Nate Brandt

Printed in the United States of America
First Edition 2017
6 7 8 9 10 11 12 13 14 15

09/20/2018

*Special thanks to:*

*Jim Burns, Ph.D for guidance and consultation on having conversations about sexual integrity*

*Jon Acuff for guidance and consultation on having conversations about technological responsibility*

*Jean Sumner, MD for guidance and consultation on having conversations about healthy habits*

*Every educator, counselor, community leader, and researcher who invested in the Phase Project*

# TABLE OF CONTENTS

HOW TO USE THIS GUIDE .......................................... pg. 9

## 52 WEEKS
TO PARENT YOUR KINDERGARTNER ................. pg. 11

**pg. 12 MEASURE YOUR WEEKS**      **pg. 20 DISCOVER THIS PHASE**

## SIX THINGS
EVERY KID NEEDS ...................................................... pg. 29

**pg. 32 LOVE**
ONE QUESTION YOUR
KINDERGARTNER IS ASKING

**pg. 50 FUN**
WAYS TO HAVE FUN WITH
YOUR KINDERGARTNER

**pg. 38 STORIES**
BOOKS TO READ
WITH YOUR KINDERGARTNER

**pg. 56 TRIBES**
ADULTS WHO MIGHT INFLUENCE
YOUR KINDERGARTNER

**pg. 44 WORK**
WORK YOUR KINDERGARTNER
CAN DO

**pg. 62 WORDS**
WORDS YOUR KINDERGARTNER
NEEDS TO HEAR

## FOUR CONVERSATIONS
TO HAVE IN THIS PHASE ..................................... pg. 69

**pg. 72 HEALTH**
DEVELOP POSITIVE ROUTINES

**pg. 84 TECHNOLOGY**
EXPLORE THE POSSIBILITIES

**pg. 78 SEX**
INFORM THEM HOW
THINGS WORK

**pg. 90 FAITH**
PROVOKE DISCOVERY

THE RHYTHM OF YOUR WEEK ........................... pg. 96

PHASE LIFE MAP OVERVIEW ............................... pg. 106

# HOW TO USE THIS ~~BOOK~~ ~~JOURNAL~~ GUIDE

The guide you hold in your hand doesn't have very many words, but it does have a lot of ideas. Some of these ideas come from thousands of hours of research. Others come from parents, educators, and volunteers who spend every day with kids the same age as yours. This guide won't tell you everything about your kid, but it will tell you a few things about kids at this age.

The best way to use this guide is to take what these pages tell you about kindergartners and combine it with what you know is true about *your* kindergartner.

Let's sum it up:

**THINGS ABOUT KINDERGARTNERS +**
**THOUGHTS ABOUT *YOUR* KINDERGARTNER =**
**YOUR GUIDE TO THE NEXT 52 WEEKS OF PARENTING**

After each idea in this guide, there are pages with a few questions designed to prompt you to think about your kid, your family, and yourself as a parent. The only guarantee we give to parents who use this guide is this: You will mess up some things as a parent this year. Actually, that's a guarantee to every parent, regardless. But you, you picked up this book! You want to be a better parent. And that's what we hope this guide will do: help you parent your kid just a little better, simply because you paused to consider a few ideas that can help you make the most of this phase.

# 52 WEEKS

## —

## TO PARENT YOUR KINDERGARTNER

WHEN YOU SEE
HOW MUCH

*Time*

YOU HAVE LEFT

—

YOU TEND TO DO

*More*

WITH THE TIME
YOU HAVE NOW.

THERE ARE APPROXIMATELY

# 936 WEEKS

FROM THE TIME A BABY IS BORN
UNTIL THEY GROW UP AND MOVE TO
WHATEVER IS NEXT.

It may seem hard to believe, but on the day your child starts kindergarten, you only have 676 weeks remaining. And while things like cell phone contracts and learner's permits still feel far away, your kid is growing up faster than you ever dreamed.

That's why every week counts. Of course, each week might not feel significant. There may be weeks this year when all you feel like you accomplished was waking them (and you) up early enough to get them to school on time. That's okay.

Take a deep breath.
You don't have to get everything done this week.

But what happens in your child's life week after week, year after year, adds up over time. So, it might be a good idea to put a number to your weeks.

## MEASURE IT OUT.

Write down the number of weeks that have already passed since your child was born. Then write down the number of weeks you have left before they graduate high school.

🔑 **HINT:** If you want a little help counting it out, you can download the free Parent Cue app on all mobile platforms.

_____

_____

_____

## CREATE A VISUAL COUNTDOWN.

Find a jar and fill it with one marble for each week you have remaining with your child. Then make a habit of removing one marble every week as a reminder to make the most of your time. Where can you place your visual countdown so you will see it frequently?

_____

_____

_____

_____

_____

Which day of the week is best for you to remove a marble?

_____

_____

_____

Is there anything you want to do each week as you remove a marble? *(Examples: say a prayer, play a game, retell one favorite memory from this past week)*

_____

_____

_____

_____

_____

_____

_____

_____

_____

_____

_____

_____

EVERY PHASE IS A
TIMEFRAME
IN A KID'S LIFE
WHEN YOU CAN
LEVERAGE
DISTINCTIVE
OPPORTUNITIES
TO INFLUENCE
THEIR
*future.*

# YOU ONLY HAVE
# 52 WEEKS
## WITH YOUR KINDERGARTNER

*while they are still in kindergarten.*

Then they will be in first grade,

*and you will never know them as a kindergartner again.*

---

Or to say it another way:

Before you know it, your kid will grow up a little more and . . .

play on a sports team.

legitimately beat you at checkers.

stop sitting in your lap (if they haven't already).

---

The point is this: The phase you are in now has remarkable potential. And before the end of kindergarten, there are some distinctive opportunities you don't want to miss. So as you count down the next 52 weeks, pay attention to what makes these weeks uniquely different from the time you've already spent together and the weeks you will have when they move on to the next phase.

**What are some things you have noticed about your kindergartner in this phase that you really enjoy?**

_____

_____

_____

_____

_____

_____

_____

_____

_____

_____

_____

_____

_____

_____

_____

_____

_____

_____

_____

_____

**What is something new you are learning as a parent during this phase?**

_____

_____

_____

_____

_____

_____

_____

_____

_____

_____

_____

_____

_____

_____

_____

_____

_____

_____

_____

# KINDERGARTEN

—

THE PHASE WHEN UNFILTERED WORDS MAKE YOU LAUGH, SCHOOL DROP-OFF MAKES YOU CRY, AND LIFE BECOMES A STAGE WHERE YOUR KID SHOUTS,

*"Look at me!"*

## GET READY FOR MEMORABLE STATEMENTS.

By this age, a child can speak in sentences . . . and long, wandering monologues. But you will be amazed and entertained by all the profound and uncensored things they say, like, "How did you get the wrinkles out of your hair?" and, "You're talking so much I can't hear you."

## ADJUST FOR A CULTURAL SHIFT: SCHOOL.

This means less time for play, more early-morning alarm clocks, and a higher demand for focused attention. While kids at this age thrive on routine and predictability, they also crave opportunities to have a little unstructured play, a chance to skip and run, to throw and catch, and to use their imagination.

## GIVE SOME UNDIVIDED ATTENTION.

While previously a kid might have been one adorable toddler drawing the attention of multiple adults, they are now in a classroom with multiple kids—some even as cute and as smart as they are. At school, at church, or on the soccer field, one thing is true: They want your undivided attention. So give it as often as possible.

THIS

YEAR

YOUR

KINDER-

GARTNER

IS

*changing.*

# PHYSICALLY

- Loses incisor teeth (6-8 years)
- Grows two to three inches and gains an average of five pounds
- Able to ride a bicycle, roller skate, and jump rope
- Draws a person with a body
- Needs 10-12 hours of sleep each night

# SOCIALLY

- Wants to please and help adults
- Has a hard time asking for help
- Needs guidance taking turns and losing well
- May show some (not much) gender preference for playmates

# MENTALLY

- Can focus on one activity for 5-15 minutes
- Recognizes and names numbers, shapes, and colors
- Knows the difference between need vs. want and real vs. pretend
- Doesn't logically interpret cause and effect

# EMOTIONALLY

- Tends to be optimistic
- Can be fanatical about the truth
- Benefits from relaxation techniques (take a deep breath)
- Expresses feelings better through play and art rather than words
- Deals with fear and anxiety by distracting themselves
- Highly sensitive to harsh criticism, tone, and body language

**What are some changes you are noticing in your kindergartner?**

_____

_____

_____

_____

_____

_____

_____

**You may disagree with some of the characteristics we've shared about kindergartners. That's because every kindergartner is unique. What makes your kindergartner different from kindergartners in general?**

_____

_____

_____

_____

_____

_____

_____

_____

**What do you want to remember about this year with
your kindergartner?**

Mark this page. Throughout the year, write down a few simple
things you want to remember. If you want to be really thorough,
there are about 52 blank lines. Some weeks you may spend so
much time trying to remember your new transportation schedule
that you forget to write down a memory. That's okay.

_____

_____

_____

_____

_____

_____

_____

_____

_____

_____

_____

_____

_____

_____

# SIX THINGS

—

## EVERY KID

## NEEDS

# YOUR KID NEEDS 6 THINGS OVER TIME

LOVE

WORDS

WORK

TRIBES

STORIES

FUN

# OVER THE NEXT 676 WEEKS YOUR CHILD WILL NEED MANY THINGS:

Some of the things your kid needs will change from phase to phase, but there are six things every kid needs at every phase. In fact, these things may be the most important things you give your kid.

**EVERY KID, AT EVERY PHASE, NEEDS . . .**

♡ **LOVE**
to give them a
sense of WORTH.

📖 **STORIES**
to give them a bigger
PERSPECTIVE.

🏋 **WORK**
to give them
SIGNIFICANCE.

♟ **FUN**
to give them
CONNECTION.

👪 **TRIBES**
to give them
BELONGING.

💬 **WORDS**
to give them
DIRECTION.

The next few pages are designed to help you think about how you will give your child these six things, right now—while they are in kindergarten.

EVERY KID

NEEDS

*love*

OVER TIME

—

TO GIVE THEM

A SENSE OF

*worth.*

#  ONE QUESTION YOUR KINDERGARTNER IS ASKING

School is a crisis. Your now-elementary-school kid is adjusting to big changes like classroom rules, lunch lines, and new routines. But the stress of change can also be a platform for discovery and growth.

Your kindergartner is asking one major question:

## "DO I HAVE YOUR ATTENTION?"

Your kindergartner needs to know you see their efforts, their ideas, their accomplishments, and their failures. Being your kindergartner's parent probably isn't the only thing you have going on. So remember this—in order to give your kindergartner the love and attention they need, you need to do one thing:

## ENGAGE their interests.

When you engage your kindergartner's interests, you . . .
communicate that their ideas have value,
establish that their efforts are significant,
and demonstrate that they are worth loving.

You are probably doing more than you realize to show your kindergartner just how much you love them. Make a list of the ways you already show up consistently to engage your child's interests.

You may need to look at this list on a bad day to remember what a great parent you are.

_____

_____

_____

_____

_____

_____

_____

_____

_____

_____

_____

_____

_____

_____

_____

_____

Engaging your child's interests requires paying attention to what they like. What does your kindergartner seem to enjoy the most right now?

_____

_____

_____

_____

_____

_____

_____

_____

_____

_____

_____

_____

_____

_____

_____

_____

_____

_____

It's impossible to love anyone with the constant attention a kindergartner requires unless you have a little time for yourself. What can you do to refuel each week so you are able to give your kindergartner the love they need?

_____

_____

_____

_____

_____

_____

_____

_____

_____

_____

_____

_____

_____

_____

_____

_____

_____

_____

_____

_____

**Who do you have around you supporting you this year?**

_____

_____

_____

_____

_____

_____

_____

_____

_____

_____

_____

_____

_____

_____

_____

_____

_____

_____

_____

**EVERY KID**

**NEEDS**

*stories*

**OVER TIME**

—

**TO GIVE THEM**

**A BIGGER**

*perspective.*

# BOOKS TO READ
# WITH YOUR KINDERGARTNER

**CLOUDY WITH A CHANCE OF MEATBALLS**
by Judi Barrett

**MISS RUMPHIUS**
by Barbara Cooney

**THE DAY THE CRAYONS QUIT**
by Drew Daywalt

**NANNA UPSTAIRS AND NANNA DOWNSTAIRS**
by Tomie dePaola

**GOOD AS NEW**
by Barbara Douglass

**IS YOUR MAMA A LLAMA?**
by Deborah Guarino

**CHRYSANTHEMUM**
by Kevin Henkes

**WAITING**
by Kevin Henkes

**FRANCES (SERIES)**
by Russell Hoban

**WHAT DO YOU DO WITH A TAIL LIKE THIS?**
by Steve Jenkins

**FROG AND TOAD (SERIES)**
by Arnold Lobel

**GEORGE AND MARTHA**
by James Marshall

**ELMER**
by David McKee

**LITTLE BEAR (SERIES)**
by Else Homelund Minarik

**THE DAY JIMMY'S BOA ATE THE WASH**
by Trinka Hakes Noble

**MAGIC TREE HOUSE (SERIES)**
by Mary Pope Osborne

**THE RELATIVES CAME**
by Cynthia Rylant

**A SICK DAY FOR AMOS MCGEE**
by Philip C. Stead

**JOSEPH HAD A LITTLE OVERCOAT**
by Simms Taback

**ELEPHANT AND PIGGIE (SERIES)**
by Mo Willems

Tell your kindergartner's story. Do you have a photo album, a website, or a baby book? What are some ways you can preserve and retell the story of your kindergartner's first years?

_____

_____

_____

_____

_____

_____

_____

_____

_____

_____

_____

_____

_____

_____

_____

_____

_____

_____

_____

Tell your story. *(Okay, maybe not all of it right now.)* What are some life stories you can share with your kindergartner?

Tell your family story. What do you want to record now so you can share it with your kindergartner later? Consider starting a family journal, a video archive, a travel scrapbook, or a drawer of things connected to special memories. Write down some ideas that might fit your family's values and style.

_____

_____

_____

_____

_____

_____

_____

_____

_____

_____

_____

_____

_____

_____

_____

_____

_____

_____

EVERY KID

NEEDS

*work*

OVER TIME

—

TO GIVE

THEM

*significance.*

# WORK YOUR KINDERGARTNER CAN DO

**COMB HAIR**

**START LEARNING TO TIE SHOES**

**BRUSH TEETH**
(pretty well)

**LEARN HOW TO MAKE A PHONE CALL**

**WASH AND DRY HANDS AND USE TOILET PAPER INDEPENDENTLY**
(not in that order)

**DO HOMEWORK**
(with assistance)

**SORT TOYS AND PUT THEM AWAY**

**LOAD AND UNLOAD THE LAUNDRY**

**HELP SET THE TABLE**
(napkins and flatware)

**LOAD AND UNLOAD THE DISHWASHER**
(bottom rack)

**FIX A BOWL OF CEREAL**
(help them pour the milk)

**MAKE THE BED**

**What are some jobs you can give to your kindergartner?**

Some days it's easier than others to motivate your kindergartner to do their work. What are some strategies that tend to keep your kindergartner motivated?

**HINT:** Maybe try a few things like using a sticker chart or playing their favorite music.

_____

_____

_____

_____

_____

_____

_____

_____

_____

_____

_____

_____

_____

_____

_____

_____

_____

**What are some things you hope your kindergartner will be able to do independently in the next phase?**

_____

_____

_____

_____

_____

_____

_____

_____

_____

_____

_____

_____

_____

_____

_____

_____

_____

_____

_____

**How are you helping them develop those skills now?**

_____

_____

_____

_____

_____

_____

_____

_____

_____

_____

_____

_____

_____

_____

_____

_____

_____

_____

_____

_____

# WAYS TO HAVE FUN WITH YOUR KINDERGARTNER

## GAMES:

**TWISTER®**

**MEMORY®**

**HI HO CHERRY-O®**

**TROUBLE®**

**SORRY®**

**CHECKERS**

**UNO®**

**SEQUENCE® FOR KIDS**

**OPERATION®**

**MOUSETRAP®**

**TIC-TAC-TOE**

**BINGO**

**CONNECT 4®**

**KERPLUNK®**

**PIE FACE®**

**CANDYLAND®**

## ACTIVITIES:

**PLAY-DOH®**

**ART WITH CRAYONS OR WATERCOLORS**

**SWING, CLIMB, SLIDE**

**SWIM AND PLAY IN THE WATER**

**RED LIGHT, GREEN LIGHT**

**SIDEWALK CHALK**

**SIMON SAYS**

**WATER BALLOONS**

**CATCH FIREFLIES**

**LEGOS®**

**BEANBAG TOSS**

**KID-DIRECTED PLAY** ("Now you be Ariel, and I'll be Sebastian.")

**50-PIECE JIGSAW PUZZLES**

**MARBLE RUNS**

**ROCK, PAPER, SCISSORS**

**SORTING GAMES** ("Put all the green M&Ms® in this pile.")

What are some games and activities you and your kindergartner enjoy?

**When are the best times of the day, or week, for you to set aside to just have fun with your kindergartner?**

_____

_____

_____

_____

_____

_____

_____

_____

_____

_____

_____

_____

_____

_____

_____

_____

_____

_____

_____

Some days are *extra* fun days. What are some ways you want to celebrate the special days coming up this year?

## CHILD'S BIRTHDAY

## HOLIDAYS

EVERY KID

NEEDS

*tribes*

OVER TIME

—

TO GIVE

THEM

*belonging.*

# ADULTS WHO MIGHT INFLUENCE YOUR KINDERGARTNER

**PARENTS**

**NEIGHBORS**

**CHURCH LEADERS**

**GRANDPARENTS**

**PARENT'S FRIENDS**

**COACHES**

**AUNTS & UNCLES**

**KINDERGARTEN TEACHER**

**BABYSITTERS OR NANNIES**

**List at least five adults who have influence in your kindergartner's life right now.**

HINT: They're probably the adults your kindergartner talks about most.

_____

_____

_____

_____

_____

_____

_____

_____

_____

_____

_____

_____

_____

_____

_____

_____

_____

What is one way these adults could help you and your
kindergartner this year?

_____

_____

_____

_____

_____

_____

_____

_____

_____

_____

_____

_____

_____

_____

_____

_____

_____

_____

_____

What are a few ways you could show these adults appreciation for the significant role they play in your child's life?

_____

_____

_____

_____

_____

_____

_____

_____

_____

_____

_____

_____

_____

_____

_____

_____

_____

_____

EVERY KID

NEEDS

*words*

OVER TIME

—

TO GIVE

THEM

*direction.*

# WORDS YOUR KINDERGARTNER NEEDS TO HEAR

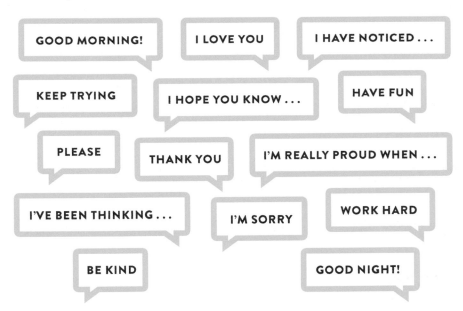

GOOD MORNING!

I LOVE YOU

I HAVE NOTICED . . .

KEEP TRYING

I HOPE YOU KNOW . . .

HAVE FUN

PLEASE

THANK YOU

I'M REALLY PROUD WHEN . . .

I'VE BEEN THINKING . . .

I'M SORRY

WORK HARD

BE KIND

GOOD NIGHT!

Don't forget: your kindergartner is still learning vocabulary. Here are a few ways you can help:

**1.**

Talk to your kid—the more, the better.

**2.**

When they talk, make eye contact.

**3.**

Use school vocabulary words in everyday contexts.

**4.**

Read, sing, or make up rhymes.

**5.**

Join your kid in pretend play.

If words over time give a kid direction, what word (or words) describes your hopes for your kindergartner in this phase?

| | | |
|---|---|---|
| DETERMINED | MOTIVATED | GENTLE |
| ENCOURAGING | INTROSPECTIVE | PASSIONATE |
| SELF-ASSURED | ENTHUSIASTIC | PATIENT |
| ASSERTIVE | JOYFUL | FORGIVING |
| DARING | ENTERTAINING | CREATIVE |
| INSIGHTFUL | INDEPENDENT | WITTY |
| COMPASSIONATE | OBSERVANT | AMBITIOUS |
| AMIABLE | SENSITIVE | HELPFUL |
| EASY-GOING | ENDEARING | AUTHENTIC |
| DILIGENT | ADVENTUROUS | INVENTIVE |
| PROACTIVE | HONEST | DEVOTED |
| OPTIMISTIC | CURIOUS | GENUINE |
| FEARLESS | DEPENDABLE | ATTENTIVE |
| AFFECTIONATE | GENEROUS | HARMONIOUS |
| COURAGEOUS | COMMITTED | EMPATHETIC |
| CAUTIOUS | RESPONSIBLE | COURAGEOUS |
| DEVOTED | TRUSTWORTHY | FLEXIBLE |
| INQUISITIVE | THOUGHTFUL | CAREFUL |
| PATIENT | LOYAL | NURTURING |
| OPEN-MINDED | KIND | RELIABLE |

**Where can you place those words in your home so they will remind you what you want for your child this year?**

_____

_____

_____

_____

_____

_____

_____

_____

_____

_____

_____

_____

_____

_____

_____

_____

_____

_____

_____

The words we use determine the way we think. Are there words you have chosen not to say *(or not to say often)*? What do you want your kid to know about these words, and how do you want them to respond if they hear them?

_____

_____

_____

_____

_____

_____

_____

_____

_____

_____

_____

_____

_____

_____

_____

_____

_____

_____

_____

_____

# FOUR CONVERSATIONS
—

## TO HAVE IN THIS PHASE

WHEN YOU KNOW
WHERE YOU WANT
TO GO,

AND YOU KNOW
WHERE YOU ARE
NOW,

YOU CAN ALWAYS
DO SOMETHING

TO MOVE IN A
BETTER DIRECTION.

→

# OVER THE NEXT 676 WEEKS OF YOUR CHILD'S LIFE, SOME CONVERSATIONS MAY MATTER MORE THAN OTHERS.

**WHAT YOU SAY, FOR EXAMPLE, REGARDING . . .**

Star Wars

Shark Attacks

and Justin Timberlake

**MIGHT HAVE LESS IMPACT ON THEIR FUTURE THAN WHAT YOU SAY REGARDING . . .**

Health

Sex

Technology

or Faith.

The next pages are about the conversations that matter most. On the left page is a destination—what you might want to be true in your kid's life 676 weeks from now. On the right page is a goal for conversations with your kindergartner and a few suggestions about what you might want to say.

# Healthy habits

—

## LEARNING TO STRENGTHEN MY BODY THROUGH EXERCISE, NUTRITION, AND SELF-ADVOCACY

**THIS YEAR YOU WILL**

# DEVELOP POSITIVE ROUTINES

**SO YOUR CHILD WILL ENJOY EATING WELL
AND EXERCISING OFTEN.**

Maintain a good relationship with your pediatrician, and schedule a well visit at least once per year. You can also begin to develop healthy habits for your kindergartner with a few simple words.

**SAY THINGS LIKE . . .**

**DID YOU WASH YOUR HANDS?**

**I LOVE TO WATCH YOU RUN / SWIM / RIDE YOUR BIKE!**

**WHAT WOULD YOU LIKE FOR DINNER THIS WEEK?**
(Plan meals ahead of time and encourage a healthy variety.)

**BREAKFAST IS THE MOST IMPORTANT MEAL OF THE DAY.**

**WILL YOU RINSE THESE BLUEBERRIES?**
(Teach cooking basics.)

**WILL YOU THROW THE BALL WITH ME?**

What are some activities you can do with your kindergartner that require a little bit of exercise? *(They may not call it exercise, but if you get a little winded that counts.)*

_____

_____

_____

_____

_____

_____

_____

_____

_____

_____

_____

_____

_____

_____

_____

_____

_____

_____

Kids who cook learn about what ingredients are in the things they eat. What are some simple ways your kindergartner can help you in the kitchen?

_____

_____

_____

_____

_____

_____

_____

_____

_____

_____

_____

_____

_____

_____

_____

_____

_____

_____

_____

Kindergartners should have a few safety skills. Does your kindergartner know:

- ☐ HOW AND WHEN TO CALL 911?

- ☐ YOUR ADDRESS AND PHONE NUMBER?

- ☐ WHAT TO DO IF THEY GET LOST?

- ☐ WHAT TO DO IF THERE'S A FIRE?

- ☐ HOW TO RECOGNIZE THE SYMBOL FOR POISON?

- ☐ HOW TO HANDLE WATER AROUND ELECTRICITY?

What are some safety skills you want to work on with your kindergartner?

_____

_____

_____

_____

_____

_____

_____

_____

_____

_____

What are your own health goals for this year? How can you improve the habits in your own life—*you know, even though some days you just have to down a couple juice boxes on your commute to stay hydrated?*

_____

_____

_____

_____

_____

_____

_____

_____

_____

_____

_____

_____

_____

_____

_____

_____

_____

_____

# Sexual integrity

—

GUARDING MY
POTENTIAL FOR
INTIMACY THROUGH
APPROPRIATE
BOUNDARIES
AND MUTUAL
RESPECT

THIS YEAR YOU WILL

# INFORM THEM ABOUT HOW THINGS WORK (KIND OF)

SO YOUR CHILD WILL UNDERSTAND BIOLOGY
AND BUILD SOCIAL SKILLS.

Your kindergartner may have already asked some questions, and you probably weren't ready to give a full-disclosure answer. That's okay. In this phase, the most important thing is to give simple answers to biological questions, continue coaching privacy and personal boundaries, and keep the conversations casual.

## SAY THINGS LIKE . . .

**"CAN WE TALK MORE ABOUT THIS ANOTHER TIME?"**
(Always finish the conversation with room to pick it back up again later.)

**"YOU ARE VERY SPECIAL—ALL OF YOU. YOUR FEELINGS, YOUR THOUGHTS, AND YOUR BODY."**

**"CAN YOU GIVE YOUR SISTER SOME SPACE?"**

**"YOUR FRIEND MIGHT NOT WANT YOU TO SIT ON HIS FACE."**

**TOUCHING IS NEVER SECRET.**

**I'M SO GLAD YOU ASKED ME.**

**"IT'S ALWAYS OKAY TO TELL SOMEONE 'NO' IF YOU DON'T WANT THEM TO TOUCH YOU."**

**"IF SOMEONE TOUCHES YOU AND YOU DON'T LIKE IT, COME AND TELL ME RIGHT AWAY."**

When it comes to your child's sexuality, what do you hope is true for them 676 weeks from now?

_____

_____

_____

_____

_____

_____

_____

_____

_____

_____

_____

_____

_____

_____

_____

_____

_____

_____

_____

_____

Write down a few things you want to communicate to your kindergartner about their body in this phase. *(They won't remember it all after one talk. It will take many talks—over time—to communicate what you want them to know.)*

_____

_____

_____

_____

_____

_____

_____

_____

_____

_____

_____

_____

_____

_____

_____

_____

_____

_____

_____

What do you want to communicate to your kindergartner about sex when the time comes to talk about it in more detail? *(You may choose the time and place of the conversation, or they may ask you before you planned—so you might as well give it a little thought ahead of time.)*

_____

_____

_____

_____

_____

_____

_____

_____

_____

_____

_____

_____

_____

_____

_____

_____

_____

_____

_____

_____

_____

_____

_____

_____

_____

_____

_____

_____

_____

_____

_____

_____

_____

_____

_____

_____

_____

_____

_____

For a little help imagining what to say, check out resources like _How God Makes Babies_ by Dr. Jim Burns, _Simple Truths_ by Mary Flo Ridley, or _Before I Was Born_ by Stan and Brenna Jones.

# Technological responsibility

—

**LEVERAGING THE
POTENTIAL OF ONLINE
EXPERIENCES TO
ENHANCE MY OFFLINE
COMMUNITY
AND SUCCESS**

**THIS YEAR YOU WILL**

# EXPLORE THE POSSIBILITIES

**SO YOUR CHILD WILL UNDERSTAND CORE VALUES AND BUILD ONLINE SKILLS.**

Your kindergartner has probably already used a phone, a tablet, and a computer—most schools schedule some engagement with technology. But access to technology isn't everything. Your kindergartner needs an adult to guide them as they explore all the great things they can do with digital devices.

**SAY THINGS LIKE . . .**

**LET ME SEE WHAT YOU DID.**
(Show interest in what they do with technology.)

**"NEVER USE GOOGLE (OR ANY SEARCH ENGINE) ALONE."**
(Know when they are on a device and what they are using it to do.)

**YOU NEED TO ASK BEFORE YOU USE THE COMPUTER.**

**"I DON'T KNOW, BUT WE CAN LOOK THAT UP TOGETHER."**
(Use technology to enhance your conversations.)

**"I'M TEXTING GRANDMA TO ASK A QUESTION."**
(Talk openly about technology as you use it.)

**"YOU HAVE TEN MORE MINUTES AND THEN IT'S TIME TO PUT THE IPAD AWAY."**
(Set limits for screen time.)

**"SIRI DOESN'T ALWAYS KNOW WHAT WE ARE ASKING."**
(Turn on safe search, and don't let Siri answer your kindergartner's questions.)

When it comes to your child's engagement with technology, what do you hope is true for them 676 weeks from now?

**What rules do you have for digital devices in your family? If you don't have any, what are two or three you might want to set for your kindergartner?**

_____

_____

_____

_____

_____

_____

_____

_____

_____

_____

_____

_____

_____

_____

_____

_____

_____

_____

What are your own personal values and disciplines when it comes to leveraging technology? Are there ways you want to improve your own savvy, skill, or responsibility in this area?

_____

_____

_____

_____

_____

_____

_____

_____

_____

_____

_____

_____

_____

_____

_____

_____

_____

_____
_____
_____
_____
_____
_____
_____
_____
_____
_____
_____
_____
_____
_____
_____
_____
_____
_____
_____
_____
_____
_____
_____

# Authentic faith

—

**TRUSTING JESUS
IN A WAY THAT
TRANSFORMS HOW
I LOVE GOD,
MYSELF,
AND THE REST
OF THE WORLD**

**THIS YEAR YOU WILL**

# PROVOKE DISCOVERY

**SO YOUR CHILD WILL TRUST GOD'S CHARACTER AND EXPERIENCE GOD'S FAMILY.**

Your kindergartner is quickly learning the habits and routines that make your family work. Make church a priority, but don't let it be the only time you talk about faith. Talk about God as you go about your day.

**SAY THINGS LIKE . . .**

**"ARE YOU SCARED? LET'S TALK TO GOD ABOUT IT."**

**"ISN'T THAT WONDERFUL? LET'S THANK GOD FOR IT."**

**"WHAT DID JESUS DO WHEN HE WENT TO ZACCHAEUS' HOUSE?"** (Talk about what your kindergartner learns at church.)

**"LET'S MAKE DINNER FOR MRS. PAULA. SHE DOESN'T FEEL WELL."** (Involve them in serving friends and neighbors.)

**"BE RICH IN GOOD DEEDS. BE GENEROUS AND WILLING TO SHARE."** (1 Timothy 6:18) (Repeat simple Bible verses.)

**"YOU CAN TRUST GOD NO MATTER WHAT."**

**"YOU NEED TO MAKE THE WISE CHOICE."**

**"YOU SHOULD TREAT OTHERS THE WAY YOU WANT TO BE TREATED."**

When it comes to your child's faith, what do you hope is true for them 676 weeks from now?

_____

_____

_____

_____

_____

_____

_____

_____

_____

_____

_____

_____

_____

_____

_____

_____

_____

_____

**What adults are helping influence and develop your kindergartner's faith?**

_____

_____

_____

_____

_____

_____

_____

_____

_____

_____

_____

_____

_____

_____

_____

_____

_____

_____

_____

_____

_____

What routines or habits do you have in your own life that are stretching your faith?

_____

_____

_____

_____

_____

_____

_____

_____

_____

_____

_____

_____

_____

_____

_____

_____

_____

_____

_____

_____

_____
_____
_____
_____
_____
_____
_____
_____
_____
_____
_____
_____
_____
_____
_____
_____
_____
_____
_____
_____
_____
_____
_____
_____
_____

THE

*rhythm*

OF YOUR

WEEK

—

WILL SHAPE

THE VALUES

IN YOUR

*home.*

# NOW THAT YOU HAVE FILLED THIS BOOK WITH IDEAS AND GOALS, IT MAY SEEM AS IF YOU WILL NEVER HAVE TIME TO GET IT ALL DONE.

Actually, you have *676 weeks*.

And every week has potential.

The secret to making the most of this phase with your kindergartner is to take advantage of the time you already have. Create a rhythm to your weeks by leveraging these four times together.

Be a coach.
Instill purpose by starting the day with encouraging words.

Be a friend.
Interpret life during informal conversations as you travel.

Be a teacher.
Establish values with intentional conversations while you eat together.

Be a counselor.
Strengthen your relationship through heart conversations at the end of the day.

**What are some of your favorite routines with your kindergartner?**

_____

_____

_____

_____

_____

_____

_____

_____

_____

_____

_____

_____

_____

_____

_____

_____

_____

_____

_____

_____

_____

**Write down any other thoughts or questions you have about parenting your kindergartner.**

_____

_____

_____

_____

_____

_____

_____

_____

_____

_____

_____

_____

_____

_____

_____

_____

_____

_____

_____

= TO = **LOVE GOD**

**Provoke**
*discovery* → SO THEY WILL . . .
TRUST GOD'S CHARACTER
& EXPERIENCE GOD'S FAMILY

 **WISDOM**
(First day of school)

 **FAITH**
(Trust Jesus)

AY? **DO I HAVE YOUR
ATTENTION?**

**DO I HAVE WHAT
IT TAKES?**

**DO I HAVE
FRIENDS?**

**K &
FIRST**

**SECOND
& THIRD**

**FOURTH
& FIFTH**

ENGAGE *their interests*

# EVERY KID →

---

## Incite
*wonder* →

SO THEY WILL . . .
KNOW GOD'S LOVE
& MEET GOD'S FAMILY

---

**BEGINNING**
(Baby dedication)

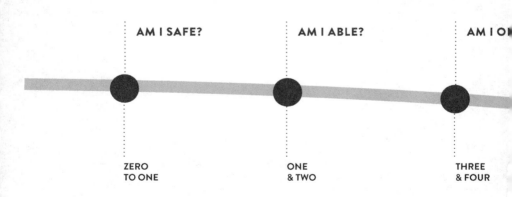

AM I SAFE?

AM I ABLE?

AM I O

ZERO
TO ONE

ONE
& TWO

THREE
& FOUR

EMBRACE *their physical needs*

IT'S JUST

A PHASE

SO DON'T

MISS IT.

ND — *trust Jesus* → **TO HAVE A BETTER FUTURE**

---

**Fuel**
*passion*

→

SO THEY WILL . . .
**KEEP PURSUING AUTHENTIC FAITH
& DISCOVER A PERSONAL MISSION**

---

 **FREEDOM**
(Driver's license)

 **GRADUATION**
(Moving on)

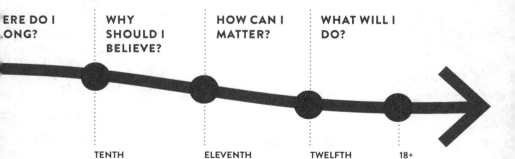

ERE DO I
ONG?

**WHY
SHOULD I
BELIEVE?**

**HOW CAN I
MATTER?**

**WHAT WILL I
DO?**

TENTH          ELEVENTH          TWELFTH      18+

**MOBILIZE their potential**

WITH
ALL THEIR  HEART  SOUL  STRENGTH

A

---

**Provoke**
*discovery* $\longrightarrow$

SO THEY WILL . . .
OWN THEIR OWN FAITH
& VALUE A FAITH COMMUNITY

---

 **IDENTITY**
(Coming of age)

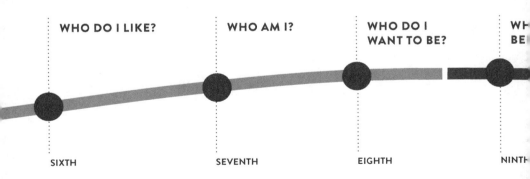

WHO DO I LIKE?

WHO AM I?

WHO DO I
WANT TO BE?

WH
BE

SIXTH

SEVENTH

EIGHTH

NINTH

*AFFIRM* **their personal journey**

# ABOUT THE AUTHORS

**KRISTEN IVY** @kristen_ivy

Kristen Ivy is executive director of the Phase Project. She and her husband, Matt, are in the preschool and elementary phases with three kids: Sawyer, Hensley, and Raleigh.

Kristen earned her Bachelors of Education from Baylor University in 2004 and received a Master of Divinity from Mercer University in 2009. She worked in the public school system as a high school biology and English teacher, where she learned firsthand the importance of influencing the next generation.

Kristen is also the executive director of messaging at Orange and has played an integral role in the development of the elementary, middle school, and high school curriculum and has shared her experiences at speaking events across the country. She is the co-author of *Playing for Keeps, Creating a Lead Small Culture, It's Just a Phase*, and *Don't Miss It*.

**REGGIE JOINER** @reggiejoiner

Reggie Joiner is founder and CEO of the reThink Group and co-founder of the Phase Project. He and his wife, Debbie, have reared four kids into adulthood. They now also have two grandchildren.

The reThink Group (also known as Orange) is a non-profit organization whose purpose is to influence those who influence the next generation. Orange provides resources and training for churches and organizations that create environments for parents, kids, and teenagers.

Before starting the reThink Group in 2006, Reggie was one of the founders of North Point Community Church. During his 11 years with Andy Stanley, Reggie was the executive director of family ministry, where he developed a new concept for relevant ministry to children, teenagers, and married adults. Reggie has authored and co-authored more than 10 books including: *Think Orange, Seven Practices of Effective Ministry, Parenting Beyond Your Capacity, Playing for Keeps, Lead Small, Creating a Lead Small Culture*, and his latest, *A New Kind of Leader* and *Don't Miss It*.

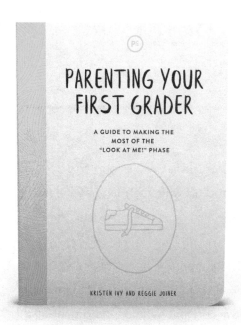

## PARENTING YOUR FIRST GRADER

A GUIDE TO MAKING THE
MOST OF THE
"LOOK AT ME!" PHASE

KRISTEN IVY AND REGGIE JOINER

# MAKE THE MOST OF EVERY PHASE IN YOUR CHILD'S LIFE

**The guide in your hand is one of an eighteen-part series.**

So, unless you've figured out a way to freeze time and keep your kindergartner from turning into a first grader, you might want to check out the next guide in this set.

Designed in partnership with Parent Cue, each guide will help you rediscover . . .

what's changing about your kid,
the 6 things your kid needs most,
and 4 conversations to have each year.

ORDER NOW AT: **WWW.PHASEGUIDES.COM**

**WANT TO GIFT A FRIEND WITH ALL 18 GUIDES
OR HAVE ALL THE GUIDES ON HAND FOR YOURSELF?**

# ORDER THE ENTIRE SERIES
# OF PHASE GUIDES TODAY.

---

ORDER NOW AT:    **WWW.PHASEGUIDES.COM**